OBSTETRICS & GYNECOLOGY

for kids

Never stop learning! You can accomplish anything you set your mind to ☺

Love,
Dr Beth
Dr. Brandon

First paperback edition August 2023

Book design by Betty Nguyen & Brandon Pham

ISBN 978-1-957557-16-8 (paperback)

Published by Black Phoenix Press

www.mdforkids.org

To the friends and family who have supported and loved us unconditionally, and to the mentors who have guided and taught us more than we could have imagined:

Thank you.

Betty & Brandon

Obstetrics & Gynecology

(uhb-STEH-triks & gai-nuh-KAA-luh-jee)

the branch of medicine concerned with the study and management of pregnancy and the disorders and diseases of the female reproductive system

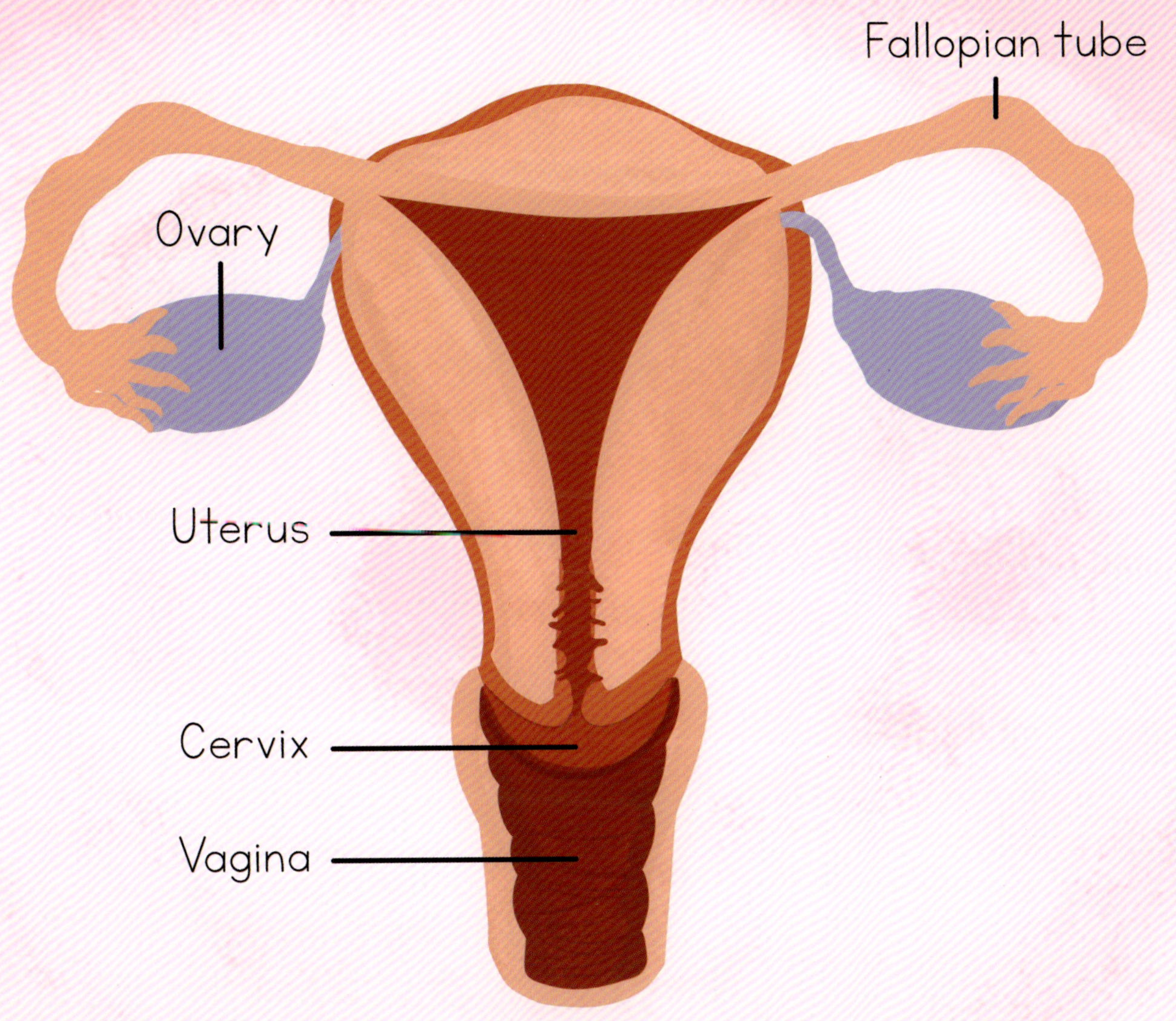

The **female reproductive tract** is a set of organs in a woman's body that can help create and grow a baby if she chooses to have one.

Life cycle of an ovary

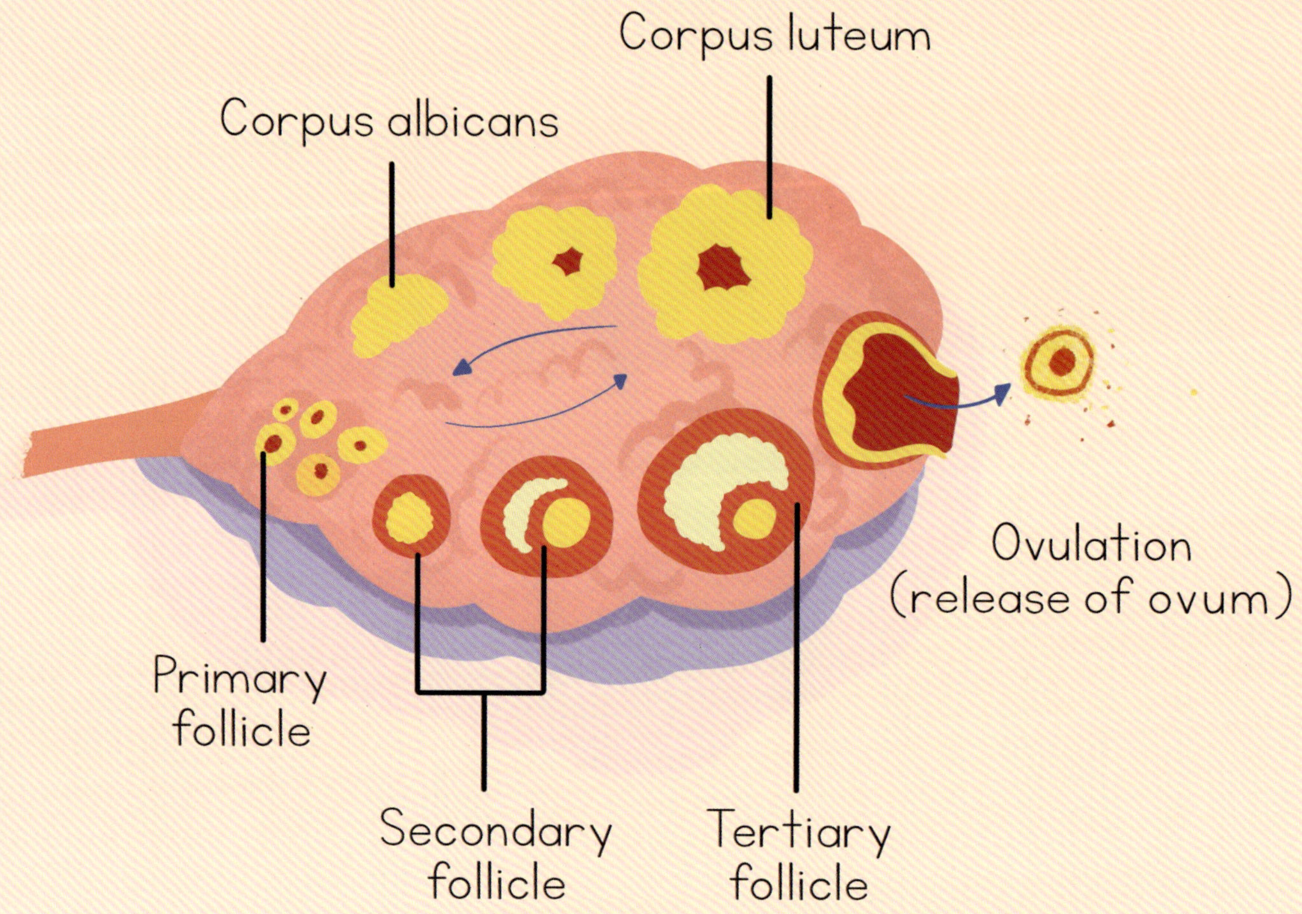

The **ovaries** are the primary female reproductive organs. Their job is to produce **ova**, or eggs.

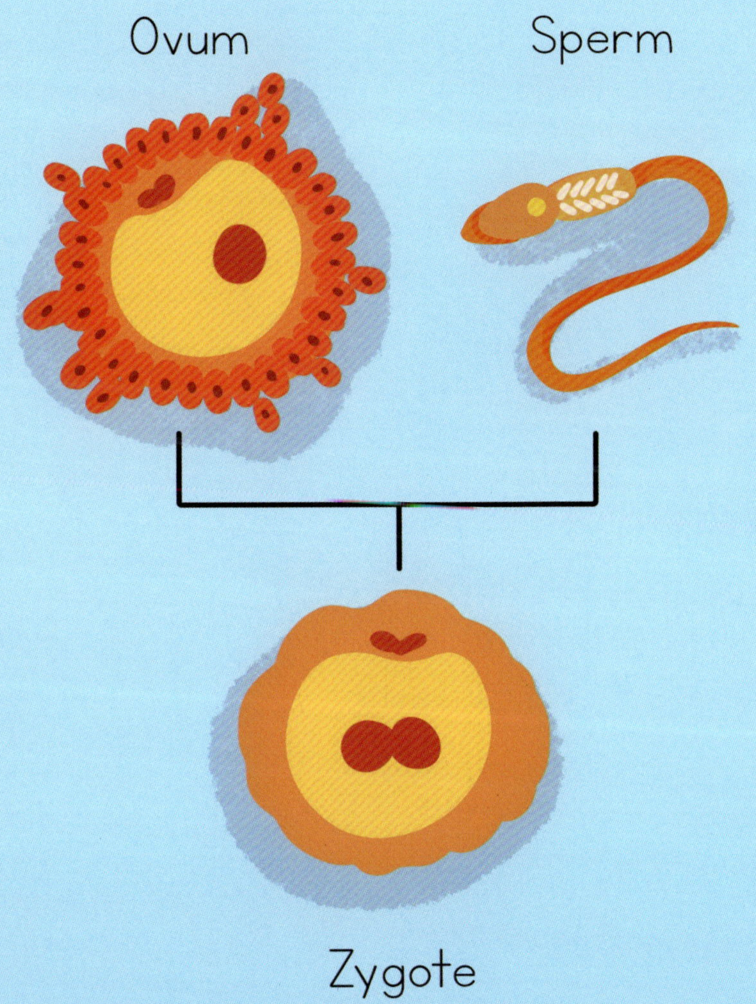

An ovum is a female cell that can join with a male cell, called a **sperm**, to form a **zygote**.

Stages of development

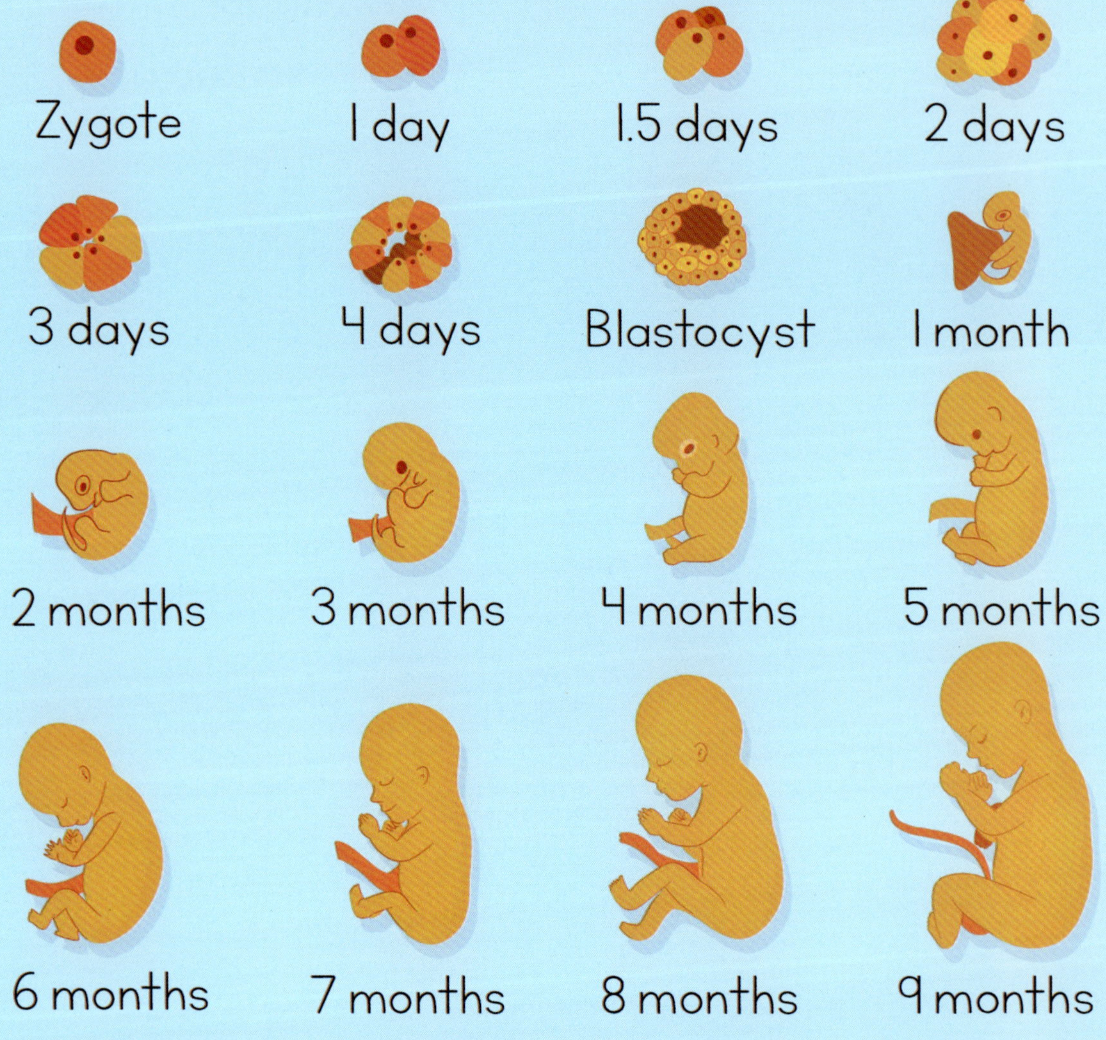

A zygote is a special cell that can divide and grow inside the female reproductive tract, eventually becoming a baby!

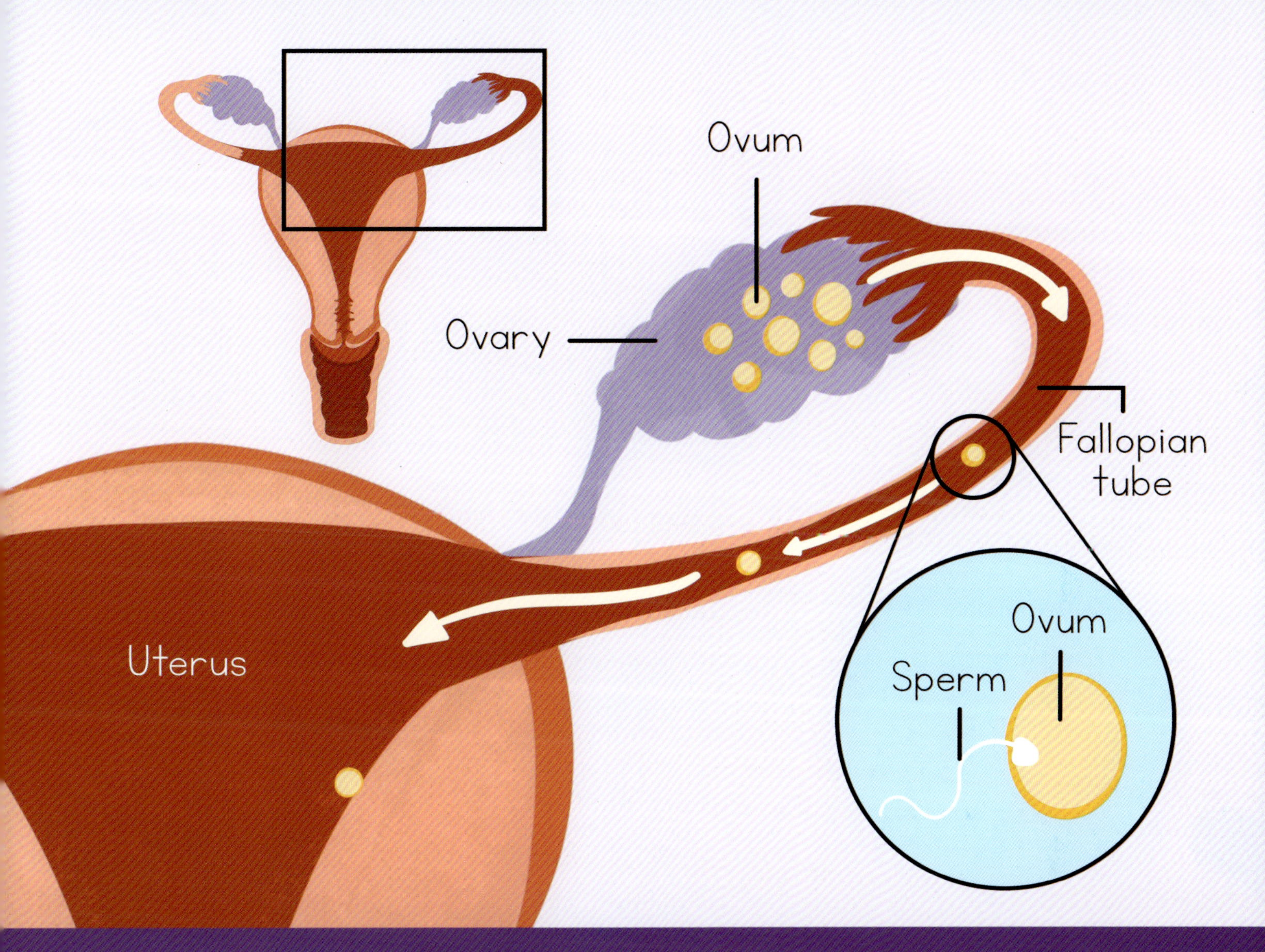

An ovum and sperm meet to form a zygote in the **fallopian tubes**, which connect the ovaries to the **uterus**. The zygote then implants in the uterus.

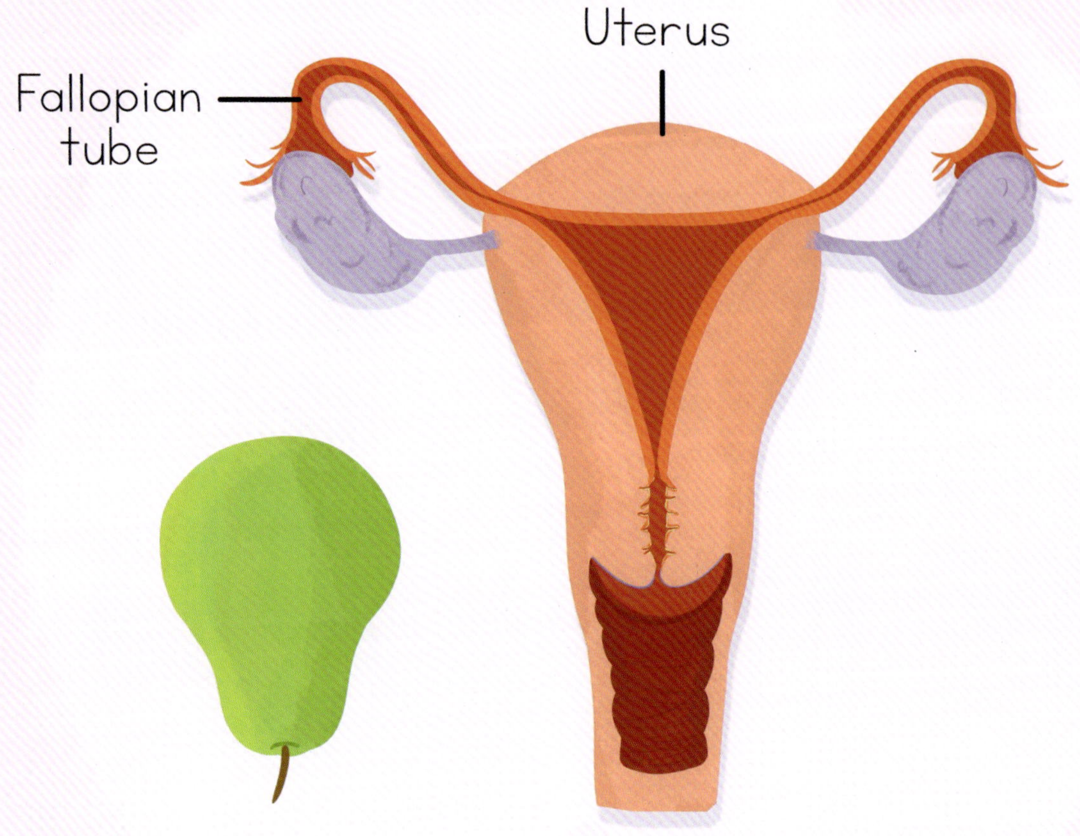

The uterus, or womb, is a hollow organ where a baby grows before it is born. It is shaped like an upside down pear!

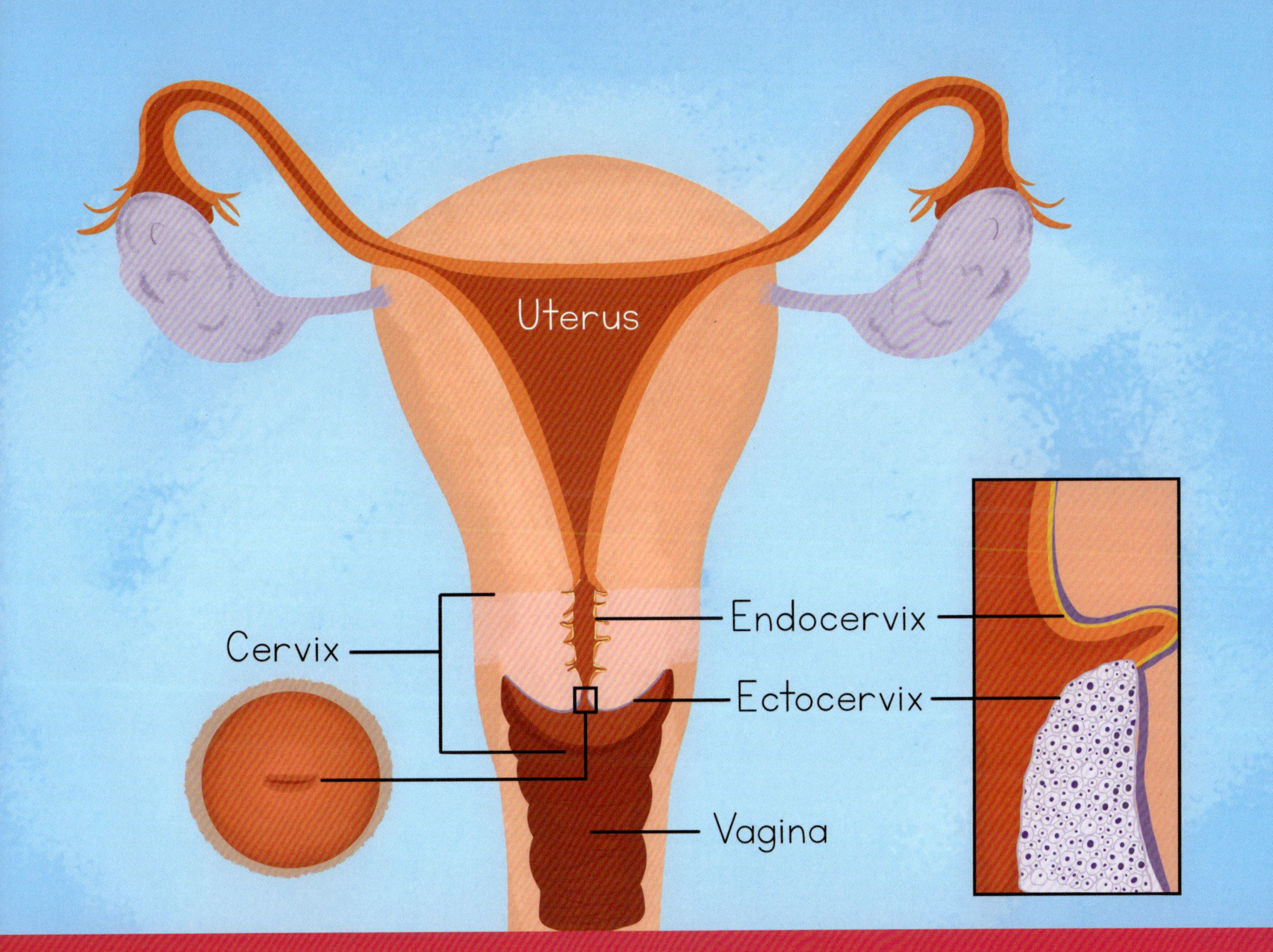

The lower part of the uterus, called the **cervix**, connects to the **vagina**, which is the birth canal where babies are born.

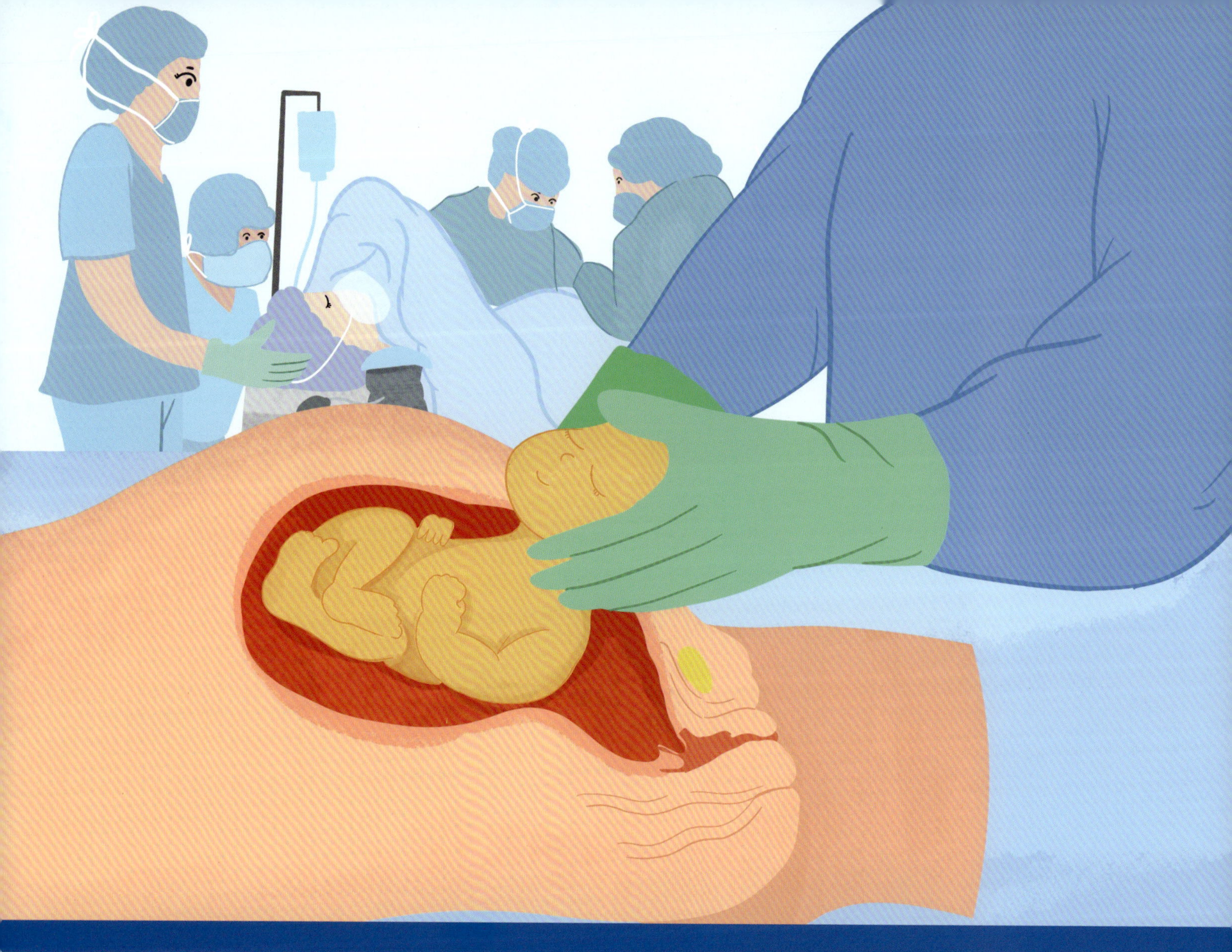

Some women give birth through an incision in their uterus instead of through the birth canal. This procedure is called a **C-section**.

Once a girl reaches a certain age, her body begins preparing for the possibility of becoming pregnant, or having a baby, someday.

Endometrial growth

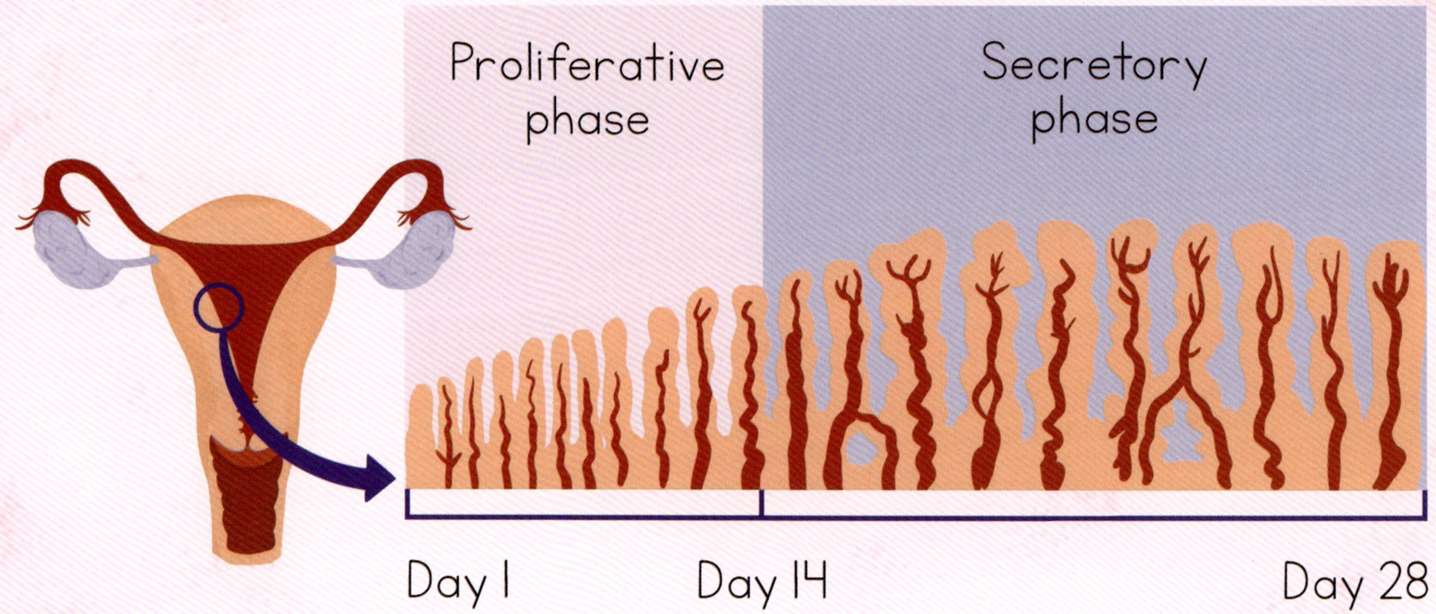

Every month, the lining in the uterus, called the **endometrium**, becomes thicker. This is needed for a baby to grow if she becomes pregnant.

Endometrial structure

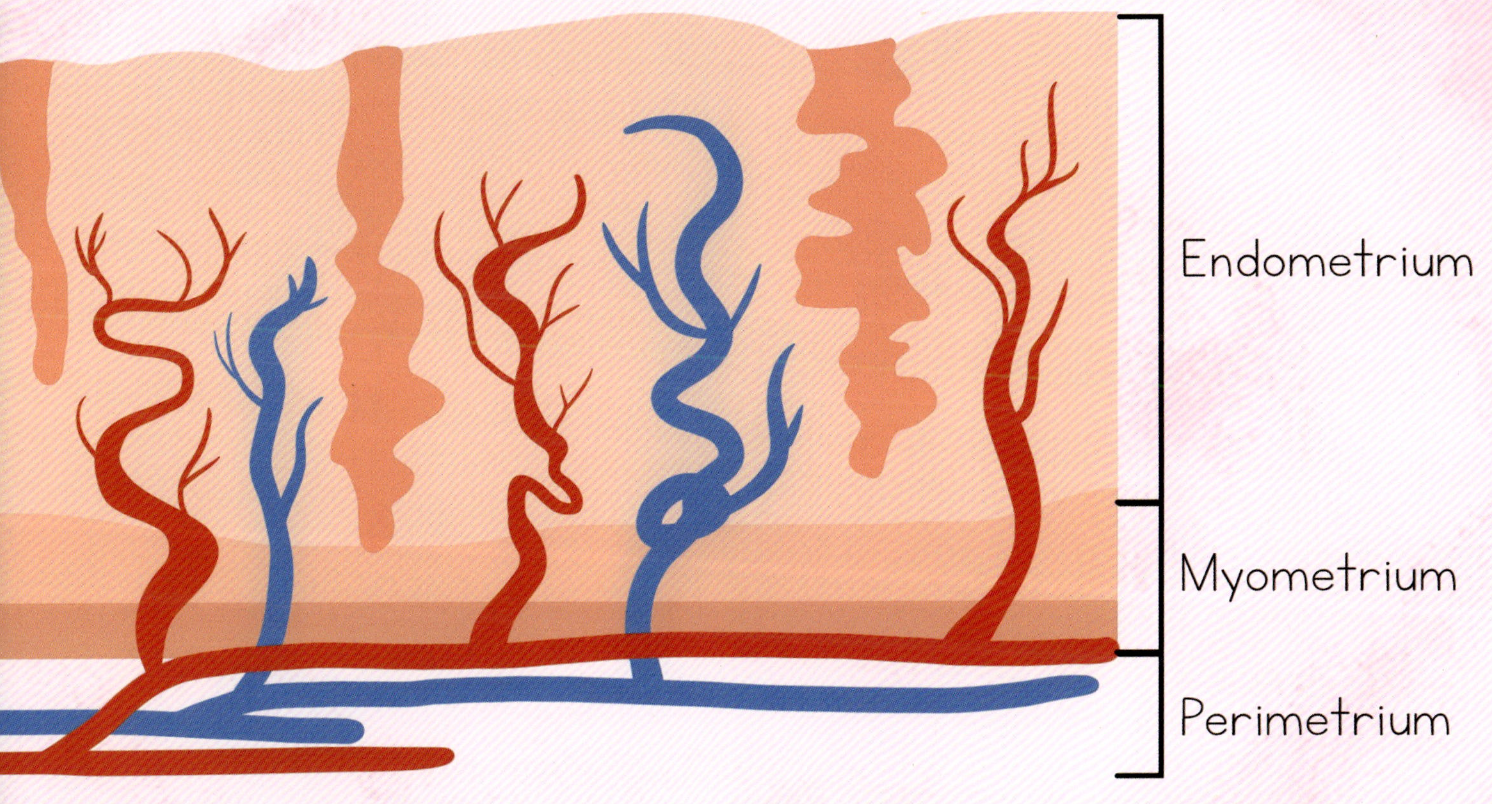

If she doesn't become pregnant, then the endometrium is shed out of the body. This process repeats every month and is called **menstruation**.

Pregnancy is the period of time that a baby grows inside a woman's uterus. Most pregnancies last about 40 weeks.

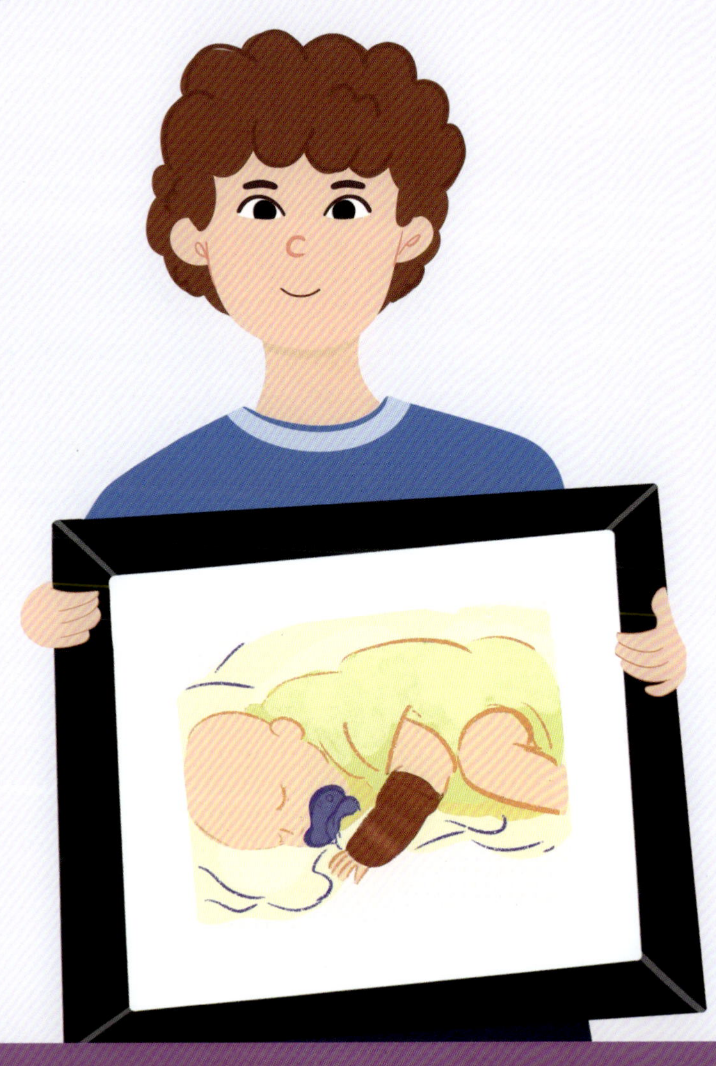

Babies born too early (before 37 weeks) are **premature**. Fortunately, most premature babies can go on to live normal healthy lives.

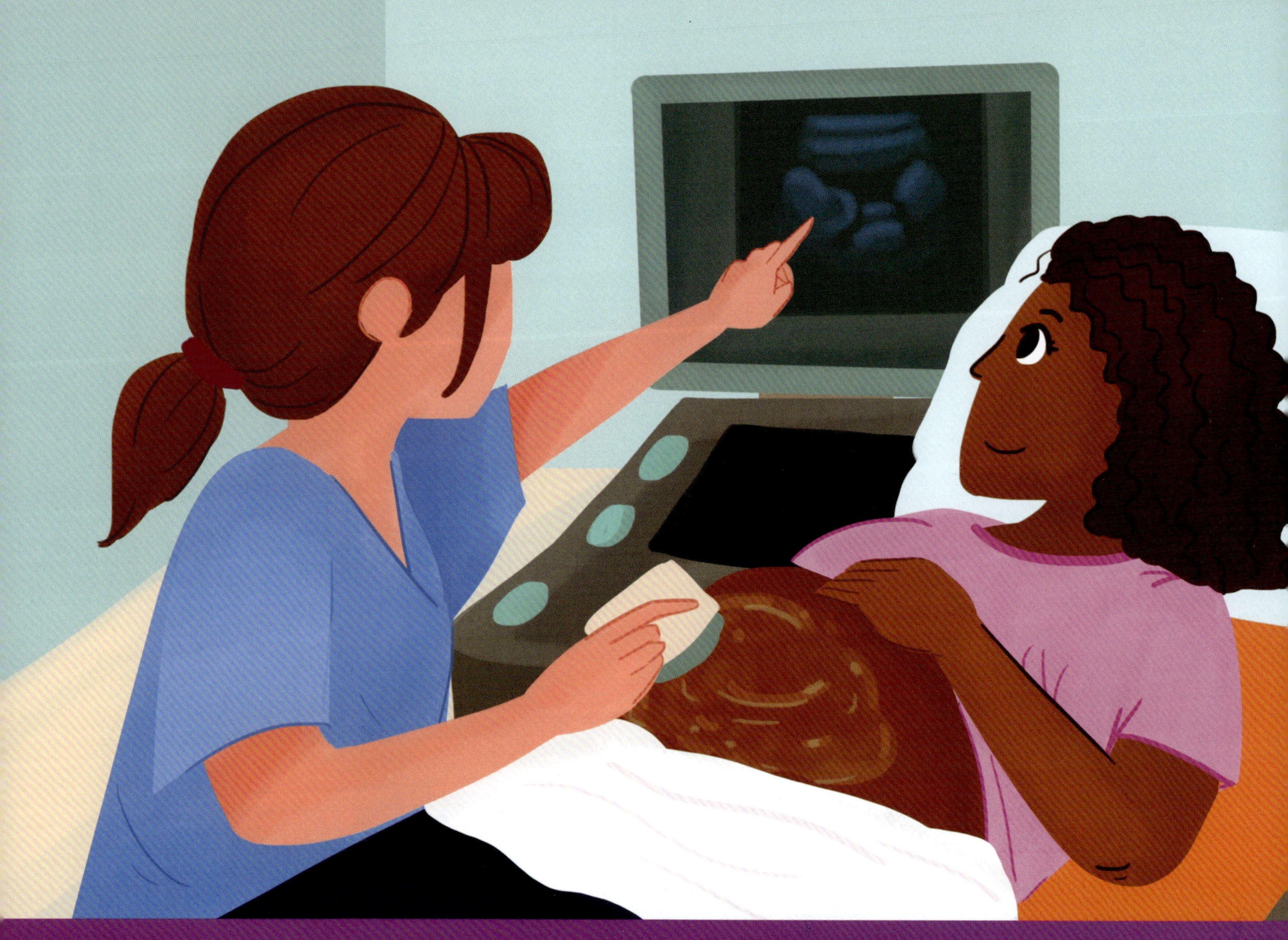

Doctors can monitor the status of a pregnancy using an **ultrasound**, which uses sound waves to create images of a baby in the uterus.

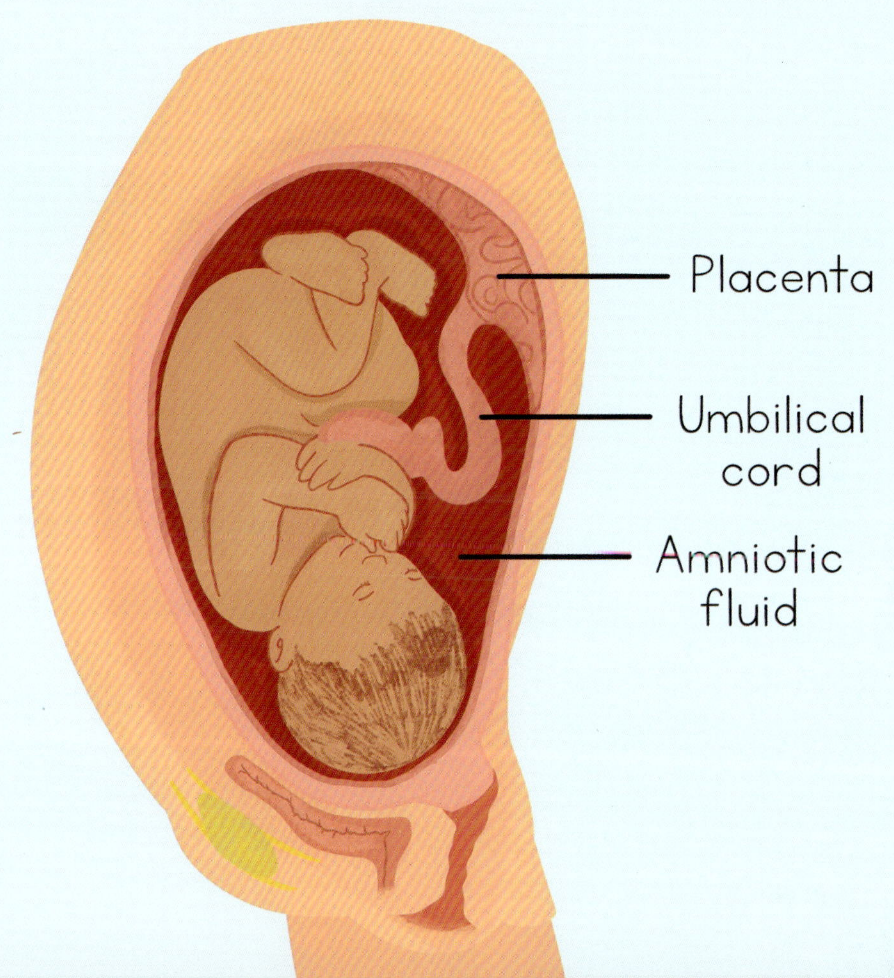

Amniotic fluid inside the uterus helps protect the baby. The baby receives nutrients and oxygen from an organ called the **placenta**.

Some women develop nausea and vomiting during early pregnancy. This is called **morning sickness.**

Some women develop high blood sugar levels during pregnancy. This is called **gestational diabetes.**

Signs and symptoms of pre-eclampsia

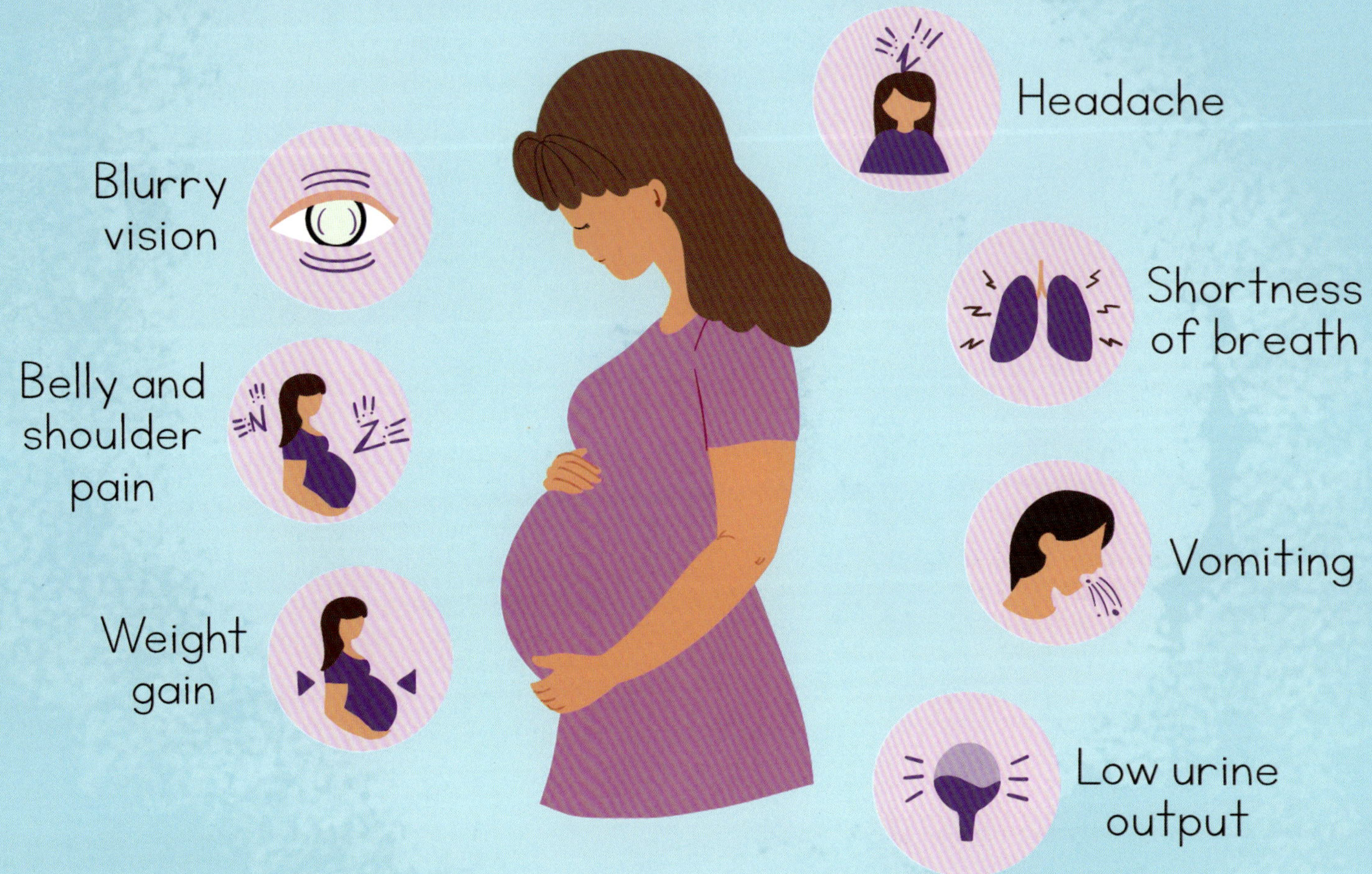

Some women develop high blood pressure during pregnancy. This is called **pre-eclampsia**.

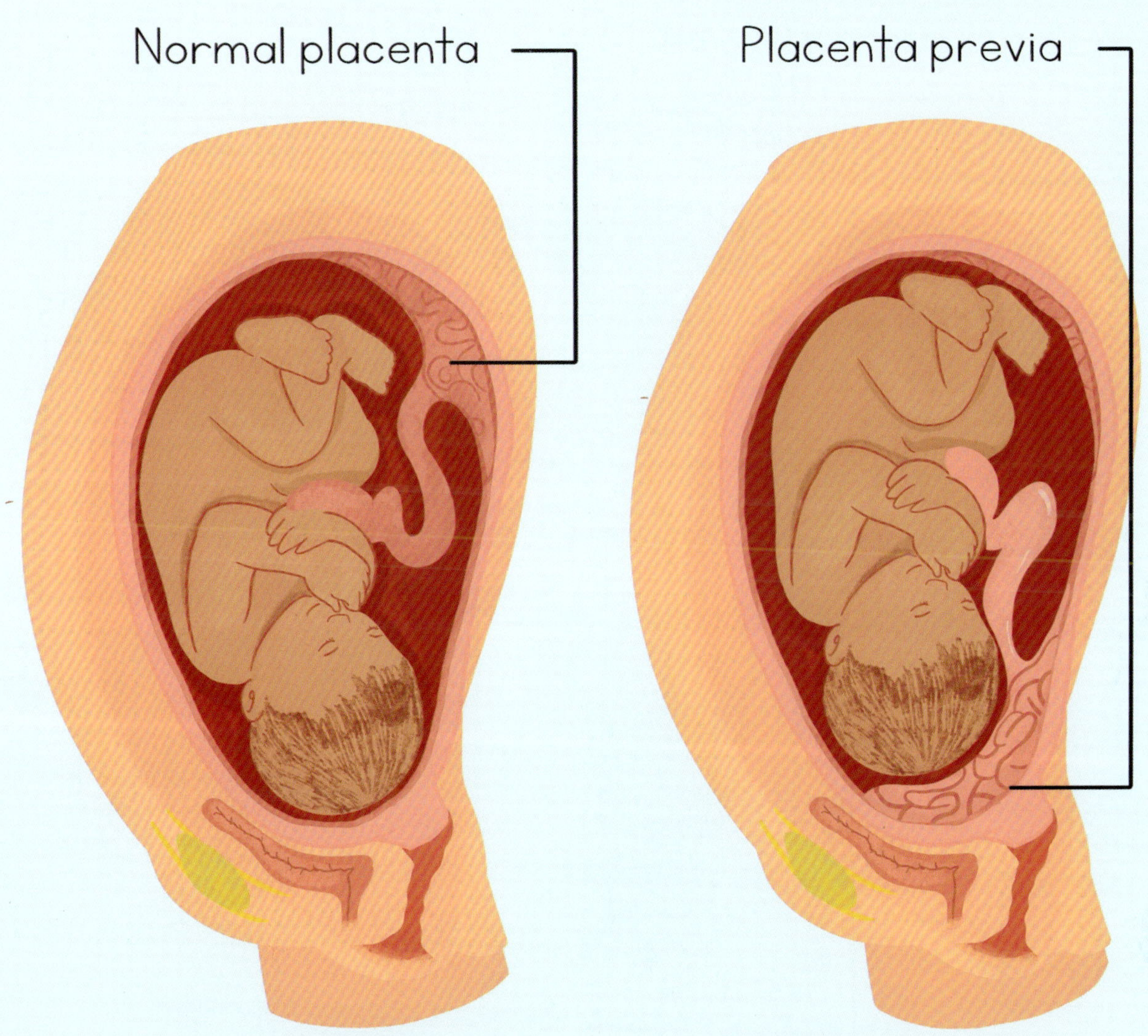

If the placenta grows too low in the uterus, it could could block the cervix. This is called **placenta previa**.

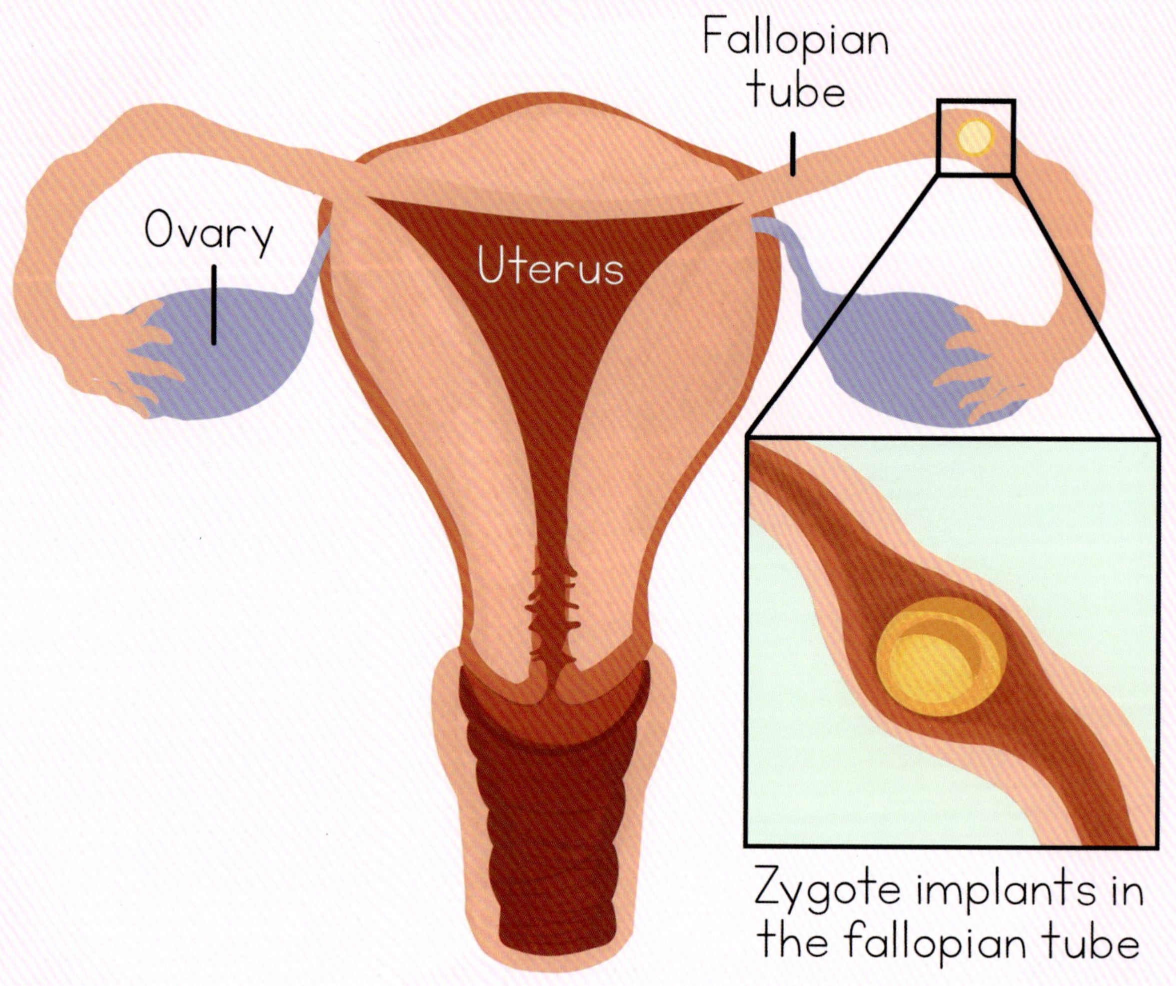

Zygote implants in the fallopian tube

If a zygote implants outside the uterus, the baby may not be able to grow properly. This is called an **ectopic pregnancy**.

Sadly, some women lose a pregnancy before their baby is born. Depending on when this happens, this is called a **miscarriage** or **stillbirth**.

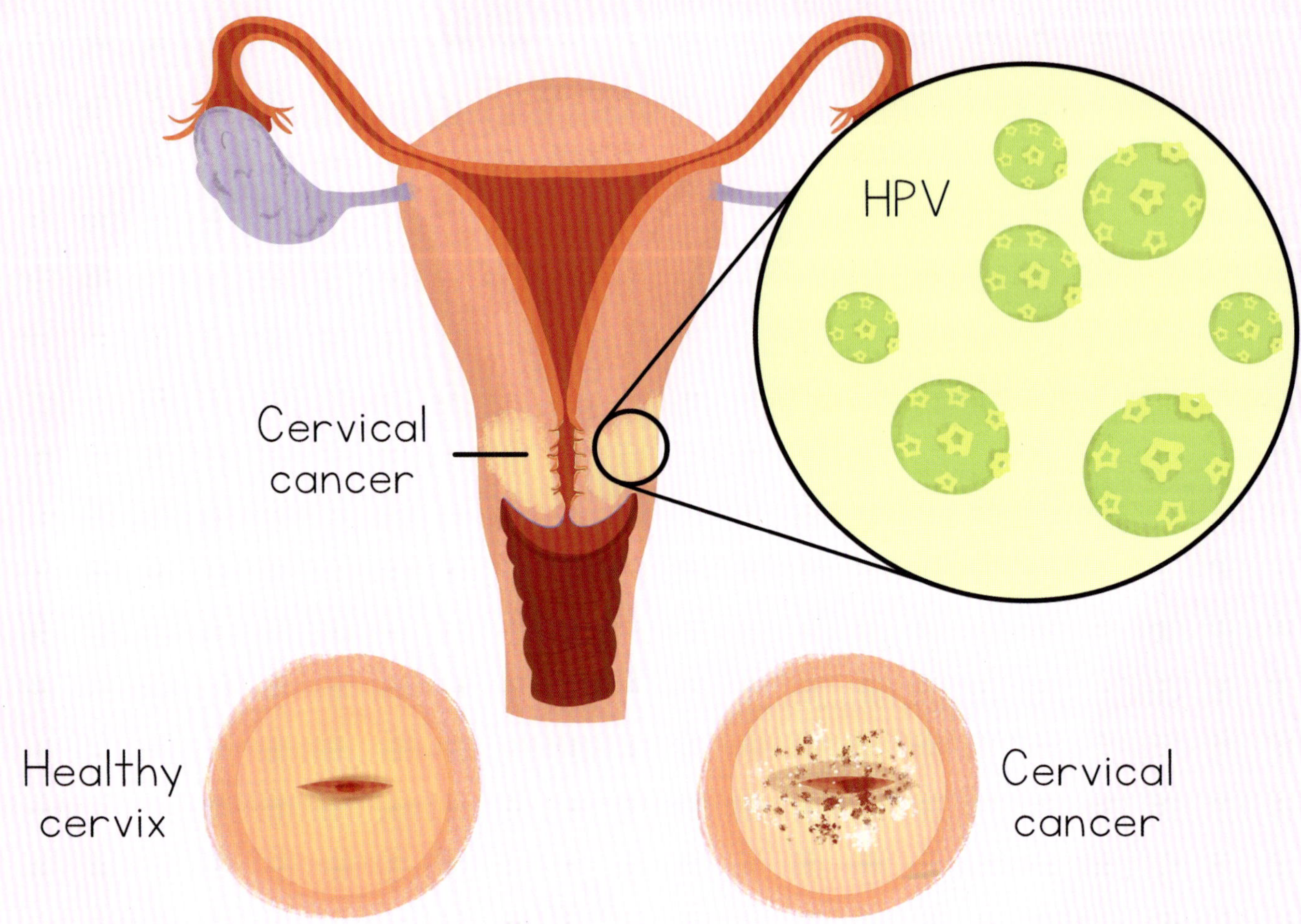

Human papillomavirus (HPV) is a virus that can cause health problems, such as warts and cancer. It is the main cause of cervical cancer.

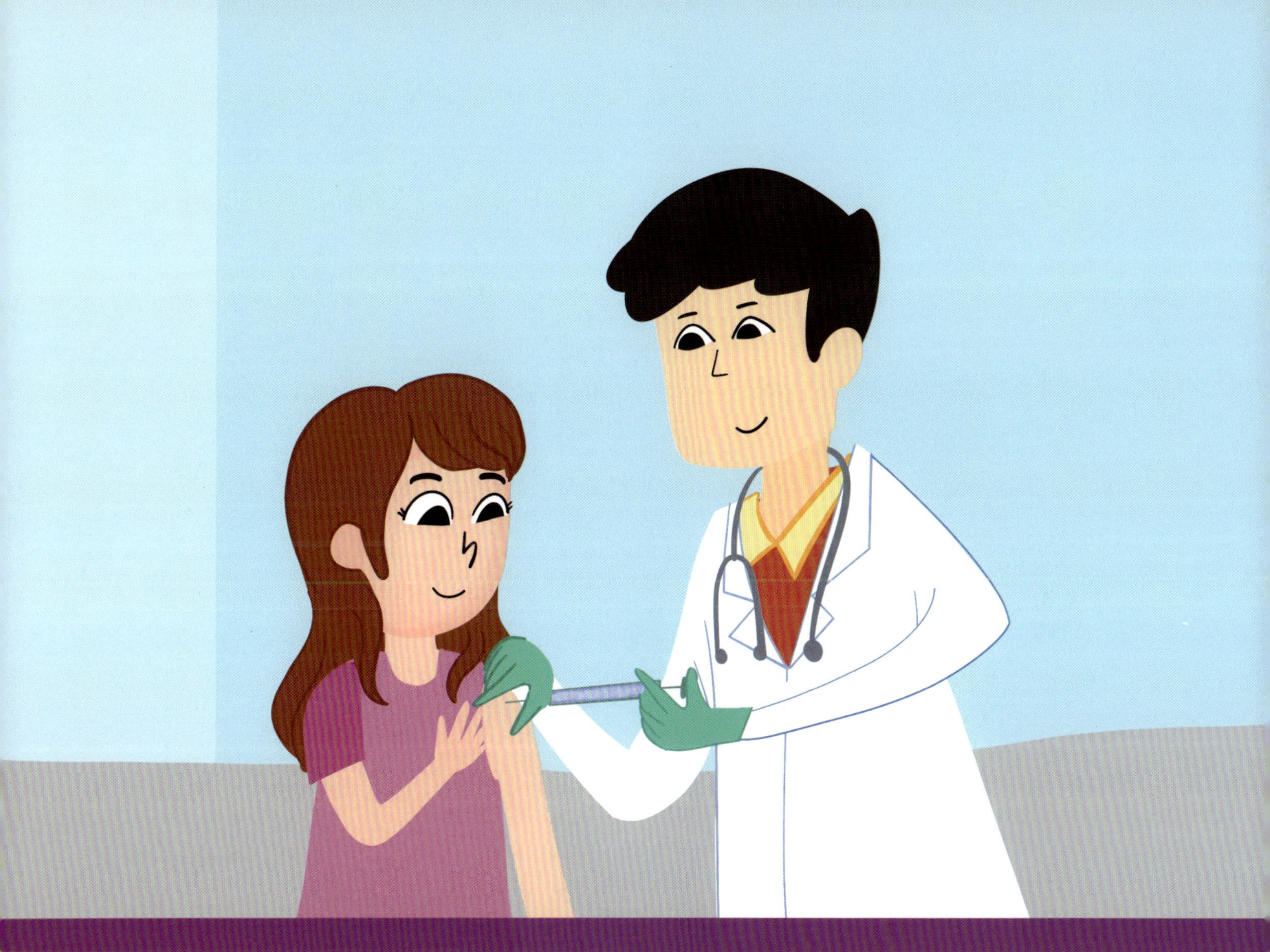

The **HPV vaccine** is a type of injection, or "shot," that can prevent cervical cancer and other cancers of the female reproductive tract.

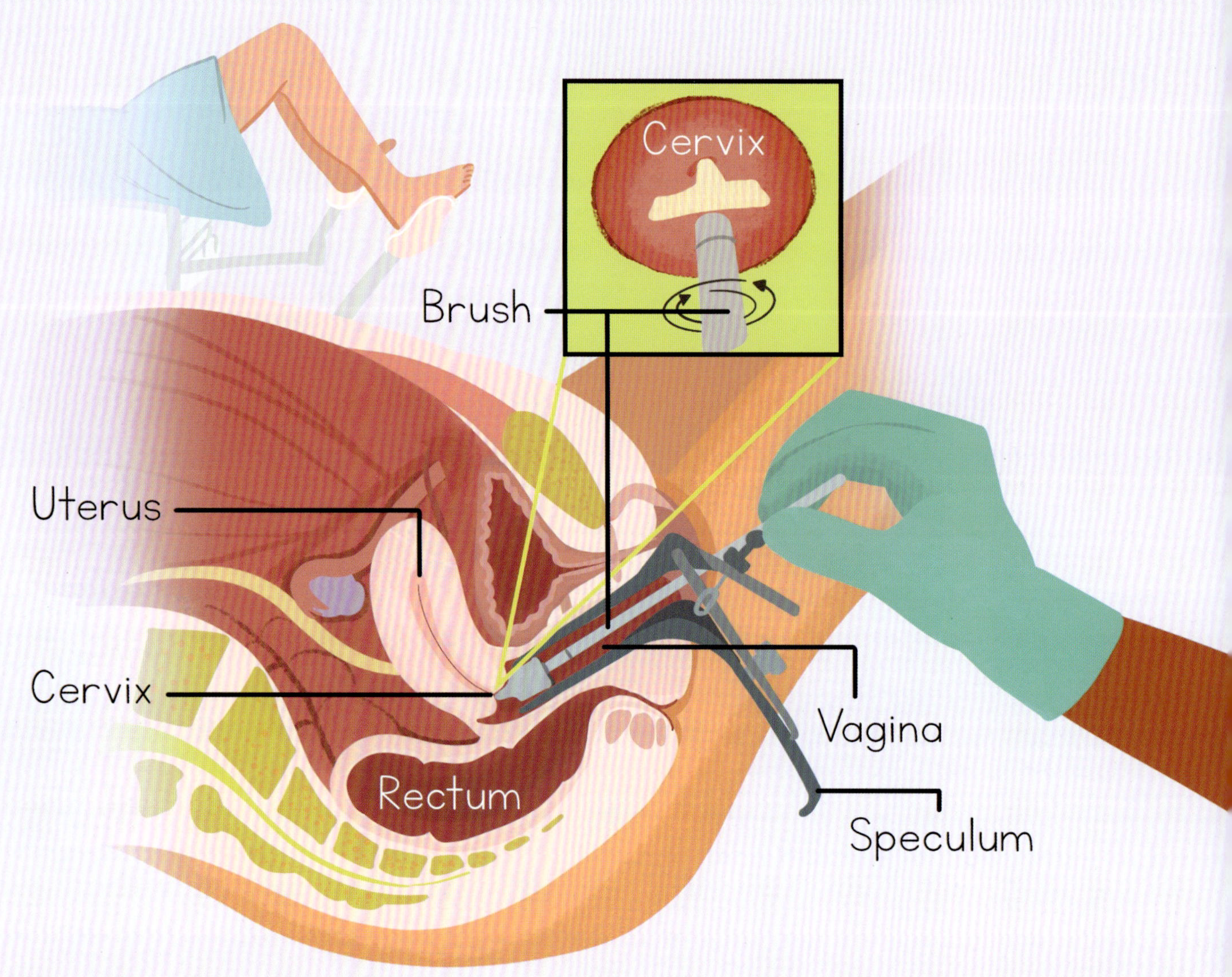

A **Pap smear** is a procedure to test for cervical cancer. Doctors use a brush to remove cells from the cervix to be looked at under a microscope.

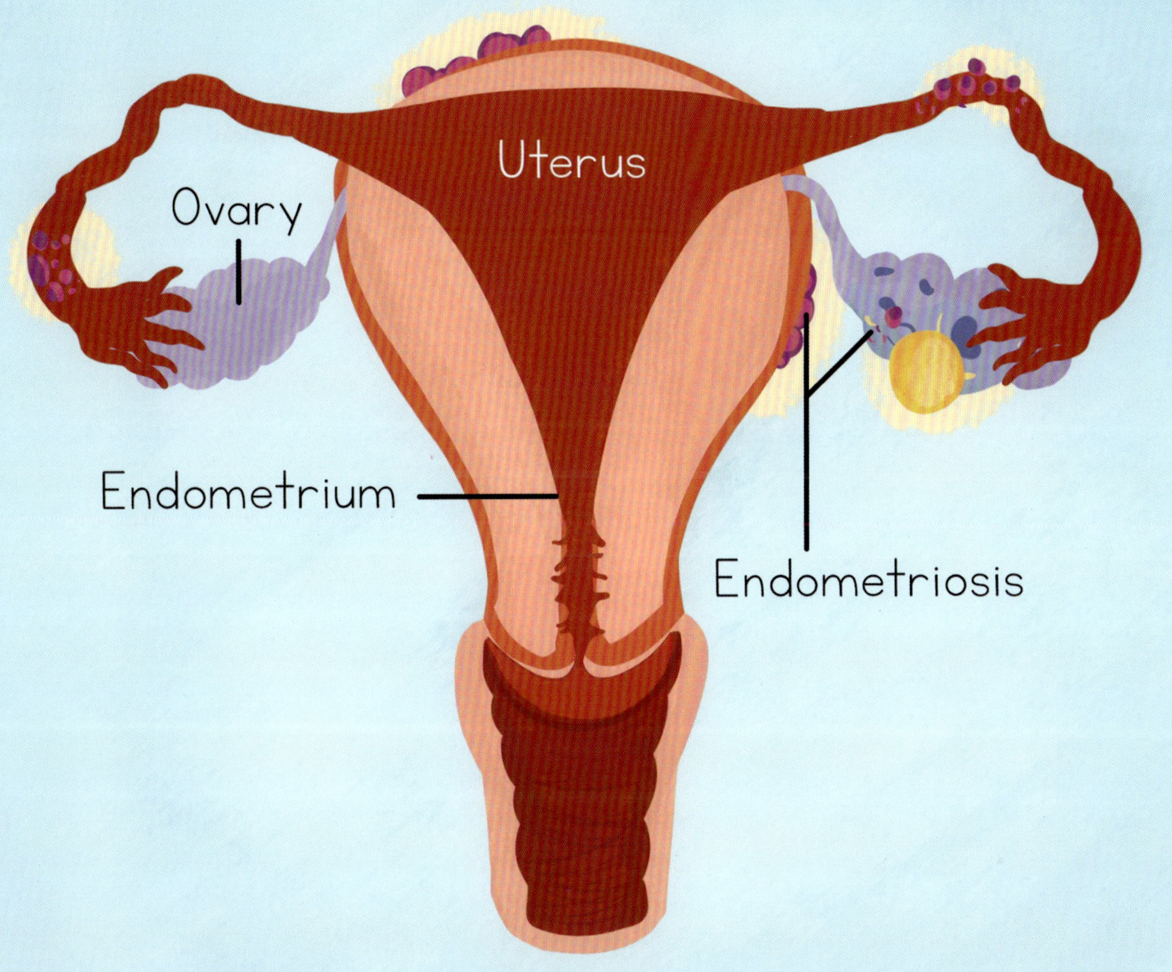

Endometriosis is a condition in which tissue like the endometrium grows outside the uterus. It can cause pelvic pain during menstruation.

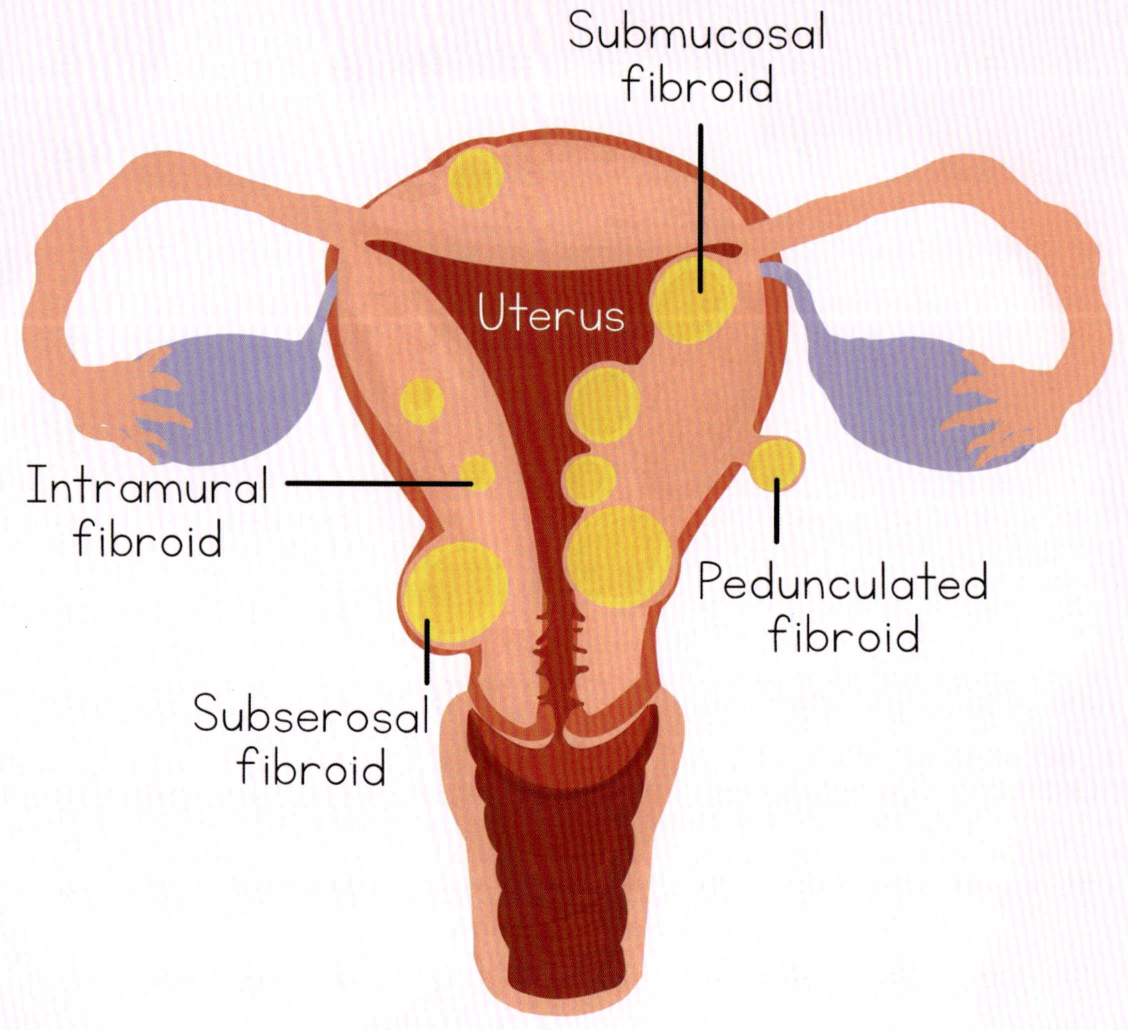

Uterine fibroids are benign growths that develop in the uterus. They can cause menstruation to be heavier or last longer.

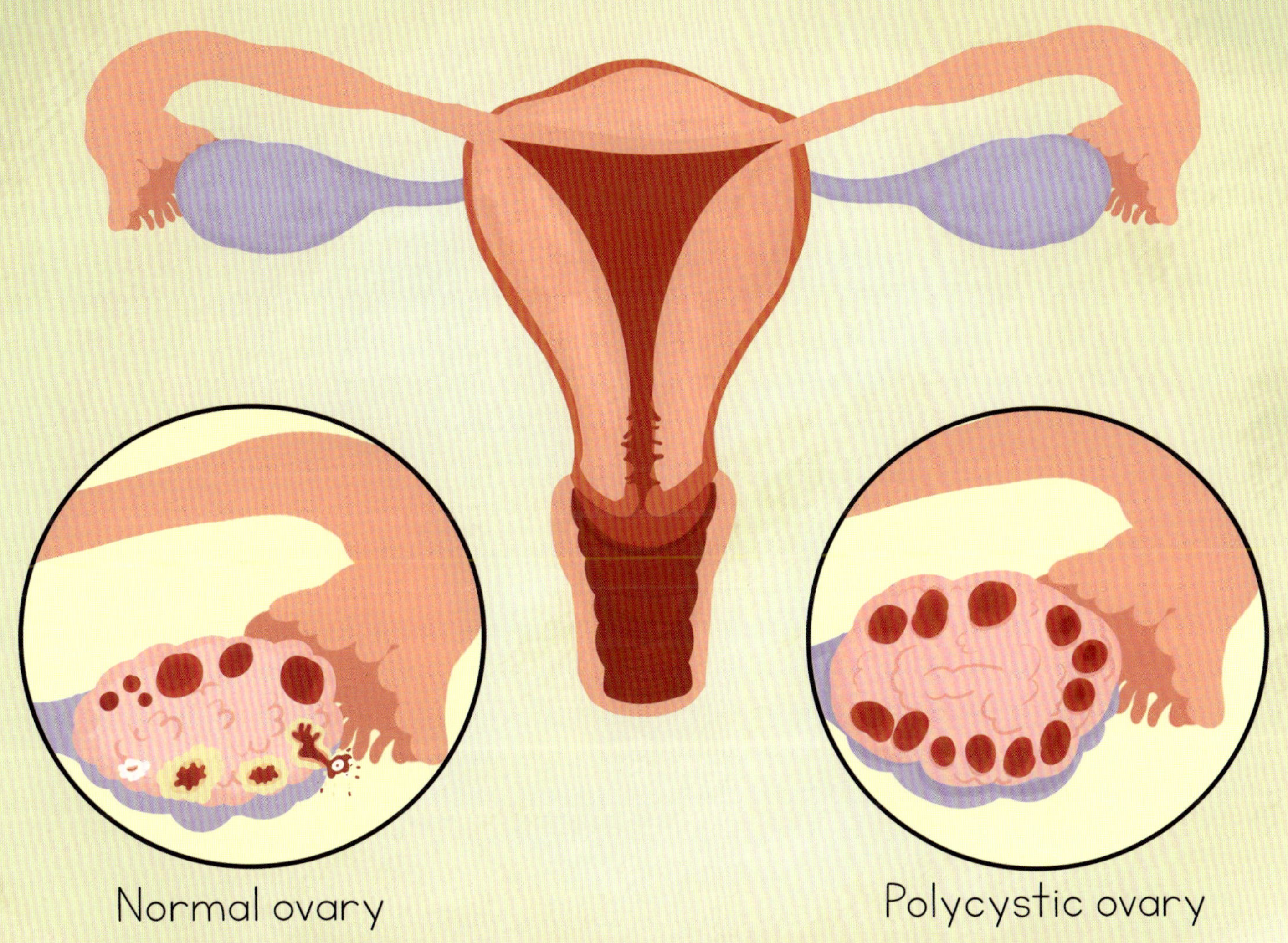

Polycystic ovarian syndrome is caused by hormone imbalances. Women with this condition may have too much hormones called **androgens**.

Fortunately, there are treatments for these conditions. Every day, obstetrician-gynecologists help keep female reproductive tracts healthy.

Eating a balanced diet, drinking plenty of water, and exercising regularly are important for maintaining female reproductive health.

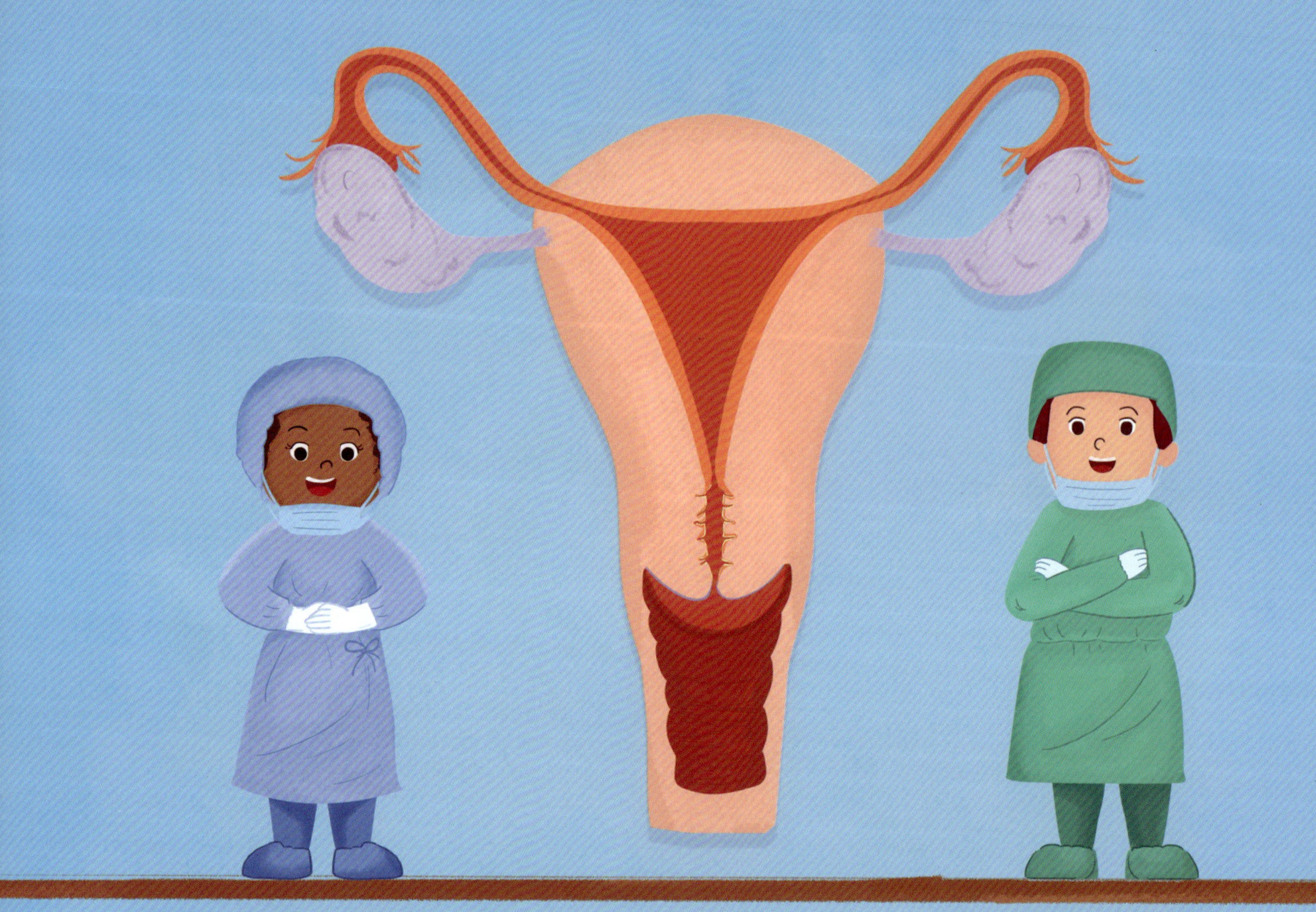

YOU'RE A FUTURE OBSTETRICIAN-GYNECOLOGIST!

Glossary

Amniotic fluid (AM-nee-aa-tik): fluid that protects a baby in the uterus

C-section (SEE-sek-shn): surgical delivery of a baby through the abdomen

Ectopic pregnancy (uhk-TAA-puhk PREG-nuhn-see): condition in which a zygote implants outside the uterus and the baby isn't able to grow properly

Endometriosis (en-doh-mee-tree-OH-suhs): condition in which tissue similar to the **endometrium** grows outside the uterus

Female reproductive tract (ree-pruh-DUHK-tuhv): set of organs (**ovaries**, **fallopian tubes**, **uterus**, **vagina**) in a woman's body that help create a baby

Gestational diabetes (juh-STAY-shn-uhl): diabetes during pregnancy

Menstruation (men-STRAY-shn): process in which the **endometrium** sheds

Miscarriage (MIS-keh-ruhj): loss of pregnancy before 20 weeks

Morning sickness: nausea and vomiting that can occur during early pregnancy

Pap smear (PAHP smeer): procedure to test for cervical cancer, which can be caused by the **human papillomavirus (HPV)**

Placenta (pluh-SEN-tuh): organ that supplies a baby with oxygen and nutrients

Placenta previa (PREE-vee-uh): condition in which a placenta blocks the cervix

Polycystic ovarian syndrome (paa-lee-SI-stuhk oh-VEH-ree-uhn): condition in which women have too much hormones called androgens

Pre-eclampsia (pree-uh-KLAMP-see-uh): hypertension during pregnancy

Stillbirth (STIL-burth): loss of pregnancy at or after 20 weeks

Uterine fibroids (YOO-tr-uhn FAI-broydz): benign growths in the uterus

Zygote (ZAI-goht): initial cell formed when a **sperm** fertilizes an **egg**

Let's review what you learned!

1. What are the organs of the female reproductive tract?
2. What are female and male reproductive cells called? What new cell forms when these two cells meet? Where do these two cells meet?
3. What is the surgical delivery of a baby through the abdomen called?
4. What is the monthly process of shedding the endometrium called?
5. Babies born too early (before 37 weeks) are called ________.
6. What imaging technique uses sound waves to create images of a baby?
7. What fluid inside the uterus helps protect the baby?
8. What organ inside the uterus supplies nutrients and oxygen to the baby?
9. What condition causes high blood sugar levels during pregnancy?
10. What condition causes high blood pressure during pregnancy?
11. What is the condition in which the placenta blocks the cervix called?
12. What is the condition in which a zygote implants outside the uterus called?
13. What is the condition in which a woman loses a pregnancy called?
14. What virus is the main cause of cervical cancer? What can help prevent cervical cancer? How can doctors test for cervical cancer?
15. What condition causes endometrial tissue to grow outside the uterus?
16. What condition causes benign growths that develop in the uterus?

Your Answers

1. ______________________________
2. ______________________________
3. ______________________________
4. ______________________________
5. ______________________________
6. ______________________________
7. ______________________________
8. ______________________________
9. ______________________________
10. ______________________________
11. ______________________________
12. ______________________________
13. ______________________________
14 ______________________________
15. ______________________________
16. ______________________________

Answer Key

1. Ovaries, fallopian tubes, uterus, vagina
2. Ova (female) and sperm (male); zygote; fallopian tubes
3. C-section (short for cesarean section)
4. Menstruation
5. Premature
6. Ultrasound
7. Amniotic fluid
8. Placenta
9. Gestational diabetes
10. Pre-eclampsia
11. Placenta previa
12. Ectopic pregnancy
13. Miscarriage (before 20 weeks) or stillbirth (at or after 20 weeks)
14. Human papillomavirus (HPV); HPV vaccine; Pap smear
15. Endometriosis
16. Uterine fibroids

About the Authors

Betty Nguyen, MD

Betty is a physician specializing in dermatology. She was born in California but spent much of her childhood in Georgia, where she grew up on a chicken farm. Betty studied Biology at UCLA, where she was a Gates Millennium Scholar, and earned her MD from UC Riverside on a full-tuition scholarship. Outside of work, Betty is a certified yoga instructor and licensed scuba diver. She also enjoys journalistic writing and cycling.

Brandon Pham, MD

Brandon is a physician specializing in ophthalmology. He was born and raised in California. Brandon studied Microbiology, Immunology, and Molecular Genetics at UCLA, where he was a Barry Goldwater Scholar, and earned his MD from Stanford. He is passionate about medical education for students of all ages. In his free time, Brandon enjoys traveling, playing tennis, and performing card magic tricks.

Check out the rest of the books in our series!

Website: mdforkids.org

Instagram: @md.for.kids